My Demons and Me:

an *Alchemist's* Journey

By:
Cadence P.

Dedicated to;

Anyone struggling with trauma,
mental illness, letting go, or healing.

- It was never your fault.

And for:

My Inner child.

- We found our voice.
  I'm so proud of you.

Table of Contents:

Content warning 5
Prologue 6

My Demons and Me:
Part I Enemies 8
Part II Frenemies 16
Part III True Friends Indeed 25
Part IV The Alchemy of Me: 35

    Maladaptive 36
    Dear, Godmother 38
    Hard Cold Dirty Floor 40
    Breadcrumbs 46
    Trust Issues 50
    No longer Compliant, No longer Silent 52
    I'll Handle It 53
    Alchemy 56
    Swinging to steady 57
    Toxic Loyalty 59
    Tangled Red Threads 63
    Bound Apart 65
    Birth of a Lack Mindset 66
    A Burdened Choice 67
    A Recipe for Surrogate Love 68
    8 of Cups 69
    Wasteland 70
    Purgatory 72
    Seasons of Alignment 73
    Deep Clean 74
    Rat Race 76
    Bittersweet Goodbye 78
    Odessey Bound 81
    Hope 83
    Grief 84
    Gold-Rush 87

Release 88
Radiate 90
Confetti Soul 91
Lady Willow 93
A wounded Healers Destiny 94
A Sense of Completion 95
The Golden Gifts I'm Left with 96
Dear, Anyone Offended 98

Epilogue 99

Content warning:

This book is a poetic memoir of my healing journey. The content is real, raw, and explicit. There are themes of all forms of abuse. Including but not limited to:

- Neglect
- Verbal Abuse
- Emotional Abuse
- Substance Abuse
- Physical Abuse
- Psychological abuse
- Childhood sexual abuse

As well as mentions of Mental illness, suicidal ideation, disordered eating, and addiction.

This is my story.

Prologue

My father was murdered,
3 months before I was born.
Don't say sorry.
Don't feel bad.
I Don't have an attachment
to the father I never had.

If you're curious,
it was a drug deal gone wrong.
He was the dealer...

an addict,
an alcoholic,
and abusive to my mom.

My mom, a single Mother, living in poverty, traumatized, desperate, and grieving. Unbeknownst to her, made friends with a, what I can only assume to be a psychopathic narcissist.

Over time this woman, who was labeled our godmother would destroy my life and leave her mark on so many others. She abused me and others in every way imaginable, emotionally, verbally, psychologically, physically, and yes... even sexually. She allowed her elderly father to sexually abuse me as well. I don't know when it started but in my earliest memory of it, I was 3.

She ruined my family when she blamed my brother for the sexual abuse. She got me to "confess" to my mom by secretly interrogating and coaching me on how to "tell the truth", for what felt like hours.

He was removed from the home. My mom lost her son. My sister lost her best friend. I lost my brother. He lost his childhood. I was forced silent. I was told to never speak of it once the case was finished.

Unfortunately, she also took care of me, she fed me, gave me gifts, and sometimes she even gave me praise and what I think she considered "love". This gave me a sort of Sokhom syndrome for years. Easter of 2018, I left her house for the last time and never went back.

Home life wasn't as bad but it wasn't much better. After everything she went through, my mother was understandably, overworked overwhelmed, and unstable. This led to a lot of unintentional and intentional abuse and neglect.

We had to grow up faster than we should of. Pre-adolescent, we could take care of the house, and ourselves, and even though we fought to the point of all-out brawls (we'd say "it wasn't a fight if someone didn't get thrown through a wall") we took pretty good care of each other too.

Growing up in a home and environment filled with abuse, neglect, drugs, addiction, gang and gun violence, is obviously, not conducive to living a well-adjusted life. It has taken me years of intensive therapy and extremely hard work to get to where I am today.

My Demons and Me

Part I

Enemies

Someone once said
life doesn't always go to plan.
Sometimes to get through
You have to make your demons
Your best friend.

How do I befriend
What I can't fucking stand?

Have you met them?
Shook their hand?
Or listen just to understand?

Of course, I've tried.
All they told me was lies.
And brung up
All the shit I try to hide.

Pain, fear, guilt, shame, hate
How does one alleviate?

On the edge
of my sub psyche, I sit.
Looking down
into that deep dark pit.

Trying to build up the courage
to just deal with my shit.
I can't fucking do this.
I give up with a quivering lip.

Eyes blinded
by tears that drip.
Knees so weak
they split.
Next thing I know,
 I trip…
I'm falling…
Oh fuck,
I must of slipped…

Down
Down
Down
I hit pit rock bottom.
The demons hear
and they start calling.
I need to get out
But they got me trapped.
They say the only way out
 is to love them back.

It took me so long to understand,
The best thing I could ever do
Was to take them by the hand.
I may not really love them,
But I can pretend.

It's late,
shows over.
I'm the furthest thing
from sober.
My demons inch closer.
To the bottom of my glass,
I dive for cover.
Oh... that sweet, sweet
Southern comfort.

My demons flash me
a kinda fucked up smile
In your shoes,
we've walked every mile,
We've seen every view,
For we dwell inside of you.
Don't u love us?
We love you.
I stammer
Umm yeah...
of course, I do...

My Demons and Me

Part II

Frenemies

To abuse,
I was subjected.
Now I walk around
Unhealed and neglected.
The fact it all went undetected
left my metal all affected.
They say give it to God,
At least He's protective.

Where was he when I was 3?
When that bitch and her dad defiled me?

Or 4-18?
While my family
beat and traumatized me?

To him, I've begged
take this life from me
Since 13,
I've pled

In fact, as I recall,
all he ever did
was hang from a cross,
upon the wall.
watching
piece by piece,
my world fall.

Not once did he answer my call.
When it came to me,
Felt like even god drop the ball.

How do I heal me?
What do I do next?
A 12-step?
No, I'm not addicted
at least not yet
If I keep going
won't be long I bet
Haven't I learned
from all the addicts I've met?
I should know better
than to get caught in addictions net.

From EMDR
To crying and screaming
in my car

Disassociation in and out
making me delirious.
Telling myself
Bitch, I hope you know
this is serious

Wave after wave
The guilt and shame,
came.

We drive all over the city
No open beds,
systems shitty.
I can't cope,
group therapy's
My only hope

here I go...
I get on that box
meant for soap.

Standing tall,
I spill it all.
Aced the aces
10/10
A perfect score
I got 'em all
My friend's battling addiction,
Into codependency, I fall.
Control freak,
Peaked.
Overworked.
Overwhelmed.
All I ever do is yell.

I can't take this.
I rather be dead.
My body's not safe,
so I live in my head.
Don't wanna feel.
So, I analyze instead.
Most nights, awake in bed,
asking what to do
with all this dread.

Therapist's inquire,
"In your trauma
do you deep dive?

You know
that's not how it works right?
You really could do so much more,
from up on the shore.
The only thing you'll find
in the pits of despair,
Is the pain and the sorrow,
that lives down there.
Learn to stay above the tide,
Or yourself you'll re-traumatize."

My Demons and Me

Part III

<u>True
Friends Indeed</u>

Journal in hand
toes in the sand
I sit at the beach
Searching for peace
All the pain
Just won't seem to cease.

mantra on repeat
"Inhale... exhale.
Just breathe... Just be."

An inner voice
Speaks to me.
"Face the sea
Arms open
Eyes closed.
Hun, it's time to let go."

Wind rushes through me.
The Pain,
I set it free
the release,
the relief
Love fills all the voids
that bound me.

"That's it.
Now call to her.
Call her all back to you."

Who?

"You...
Every bit of you...
the true,
you.
That's who."

Last drop of courage
Outta me, I squeeze.
Trembling, shaking
I call her back to me.
Falling to my knees.
Her, Me.
Blending into we.
Two becoming one.

The me,
I was taught to shun.
Pulled out of the shadows
And into the sun.

A true Leo rising
her crown, shining.
She's found her power now.
Strong, ready to stand her ground.
True life's lesson,
Go through fear
 and, never back down.

I pick up some sand.
A tiny mountain,
in the palm of my hand.
With a blow of my breath,
I wish the only wish I could wish,
For a life far calmer
and simpler than this.
Perfect and pure,
for new seeds to sow,
and healed
generations to grow.

A tale as old as time,
For reason and rhyme.
From enemies,
To frenemies,
To true friends indeed.
That is the tale,
Of My demons
And me.

My Demons and Me

Part IV

<u>The Alchemy of Me</u>

Maladaptive

Daydreaming
Attention seeking

Lying
And crying
And surviving

Breaking...

Overthinking
And counting
And pacing

Limer-ating...

Ruminating
And fawning
Hyper visualizing
Black
And
Whiting

Dis
    a
        ssociat
              ing

It's all so overwhelming.

Spiraling...

Numbing
Running
Starving
Bingeing
Puking
Drinking
Smoking
Snorting
Sucking

Fucking...

Coping...

Mech
      a
           nis
                  ms

Dear, Godmother

Cancer,
That's what you are,
That's what you'll always be.
I hope what you did stains you,
The way you stained me.

I hope it eats you
from the inside out.
I hope you drown in it.
I hope it drags you down.
I hope you scream in agony,
And no one hears a fucking sound.

I hope you collapse
under the full weight of
Shame and grief
I hope you fall to your knees
I hope you beg and you plead,
To god … even the ones,
you don't believe…
I hope they all say,
Redeem…

…Denied!
I hope it drives you mad.
As it loops, forever in your mind.

I hope you live though…
Death would be too kind.

P.s.
I'm glad your dad's dead.
I hope he's in hell
Experiencing the same
Torment and dread

Disrespectfully,
Yours truly.

Hard Cold Dirty Floor

Tracing the line,
I go back in time.
I write the wrongs
Of those who have
Forsaken me.

I try to make it
Make sense—
For the sake of me.

Like, how did she
Maintain custody,
Even though
She beat me
And threatened to take
My life from me?

One of her
Favorite sayings,
"I brought you
Into this world;
I can take you out,"
Still rings loud.

Threats of boarding schools
And foster care—
She didn't care.

She didn't even want me.
She made it quite clear.
She'd say,
"One boy, one girl
Was all I wanted,
Till your daddy
Knocked me up.
You're an accident.
Be glad you're here."

She said it over and over,
Like her favorite story,
Joking, laughing, cackling
So everyone could hear.

On the wall
Hung only two baby portraits.
When I asked, "Where's mine?"
A shrug, a smirk,
And, "Couldn't afford it."

Now,
Don't get me wrong,
We were poor…
But my only two baby pictures,
Blurry and out of focus,
Lay away in a plastic bin
On the basement's
Hard, cold, dirty floor.

One
Is of my grandmother
Holding me and looking at me—
But,
Like I'm some stranger's baby.

The other is of me,
Wrapped in a blanket,
Red-faced from screaming,
As I lay away
In a plastic bin
On a rolling cart
On the hospital's
Hard, cold, dirty floor.

None of her
Holding me, though—
Not even for show.

The first time I asked,
"Mommy, why do you
Abuse me?"
I was four.

Watching a segment
On the news,
A story about a kid
That died from being abused.
It was on Fox 4.

I was gaslit,
Told, "You're not abused,
'Cause you only get hit
A little bit."

Truth be told,
We got hit
More than we didn't.

The second time,
I was ten.
She said,
"Maybe because my family
Did it to me back then."

Wait...
So then...
You know how
It fucking feels?
Are you fucking kidding me?

I don't get it.
You should want better
For your own fucking kids
Than whatever the fuck
This shit is.

I fucking snapped on her.
My hand,
Her face—
Hot and
Red and
Loud.

Oh, I fucking slapped her.
It felt so fucking good.
Then I regretted it
Immediately after.

At twelve,
I threw the same "fit."
She raged in my room,
Throwing and breaking my shit.
She threw a book at my head—
Hard, it hit.

Ironically… That book…
It was A Child Called It.
It was…
My favorite.

That night,
I lay awake,
Staring at the ceiling,
Wishing
That she wasn't Catholic
And that I was aborted.

Or,
Maybe, hopefully,
She would
Take me out,
Like she said she could.

And I'd
Lay away
In a plastic bin
On the dump's
Hard, cold, dirty floor—
Like she
Clearly thinks I should.

Breadcrumbs

I like to show up.
You like to be left alone.

I like my conversation face paced.
You like your silent space.

I get it .
you keep
everything You hide,
 Inside.

A hard box case
In your basement closet
crawl space.

You're heart
Under lock and key,
special clearance,
Just to take a peek.

And me...
Well, I wear my heart
Right here,
On my sleeve.
Right here,
For the world to see.

What you see...
Is what you get.

I never wanted you to
Dive in that trench
Let alone save me from which

All I wanted was someone
who was with me in the midst
of this chaotic shit and mix,
Say...
I'm proud of you sis

I see you.
Rip the pain from your wounds.
I see you.
Sew your flesh shut.
I see you.
Nursing yourself better.
I see you.
On the up and up.

I see you...
I know it's rough...
I see you....
I know you're tough
I see you...
Look what
You made it through...
I see you...
I'm so proud of you!

But to you that's
Pathetic and lame.

You yell at me,
"Stop being so entitled and vain,
Go Validate your own pain ".

I didn't mean to burden
you at all…

I know, I know,
 you're not
My mom

I'm not pissy or bitter
You just…

raised me better…

I just look up to you
Is all,

But yeah…
I can use the mirror
On the bathroom wall…

Sorry, for
the call…

I try to let you go...
You say "no.
Don't stay. Don't go.
Just leave me the fuck alone".

From your lips, you spill,
Your hateful mess.

You want your Ideal.
I want mine.
How do we fix it
This time?
Where is the gray area?
Where is the middle?
Why can't we just turn
To face each other?
Even just a little?

I refuse to live this way.
At the end of the day.

You don't deserve to feel smothered.
Just because,
We were incorrectly,
Mothered.

But also...

I don't deserve breadcrumbs.
You don't get me
how you want,
You get me how I come.

Trust Issues

Back against the wall.
Wanting to take the leap,
But afraid of the fall.

We got you,
Just surrender,
Whisper's the call.

I want to,
But every time I let go,
In a free fall of trust,

My body
hits the ground.
I'm left,
Heartbroken,
And crushed.

When you grow up
As a bag to punch,
You can't trust
A soft touch.

Gentleness feels suspicious.
Kind words feel vicious.
Friendships feel pessimistic.
Shit, sometimes...
Even, Love feels Sado / Masochistic

What a fucked-up world.
Yet, feels so wrong...
To cut the cord.

No Longer Compliant
No Longer Silent

Narcissists don't like
To be found out.
So, they take your voice,
And force you silent.

An abuser's favorite line,
"Don't talk about it".
You know what
They're capable of.
So, you're compliant.

When the silent
Get the courage
To talk about it,
Your gonna' wanna'
Sit.

Speaking their truth,
So unapologetic,
Leaving no
Stone unturned,
Emotionally...
Apocalyptic.

I'll handle it

With your words
Like bullets,
Locked and loaded,
You take aim.
Fire.

Bang.
Bang.
Bang.
The shots rang,
Bullets rain.

Hitting where
It hurts the most,
The already wounds
I didn't yet,
know how to close.

Deep.
Deep.
Deep,
Inside.
Repeatedly,
Killing my sense of self...
...Emotional homicide.

Years, and
Years, and
Years,
Of this shit .

Emotional turmoil
Mixed with regret.
And guilt and shame
And
All this pain...

And for what?

Cause your weak ass
Couldn't hold a single blame?

Give it to me.
What's another boulder,
Upon these pretty little shoulders?

Come on,
Do it.
Do it.
Fucking,
Do it.
Project it on to me.
I'll carry the burden.
That You,
perceive me to be.

I'll have a
fucking
break down.

And then I'll
Pick, MYSELF
Back up
And proceed
To
 Break. It. Down.

And fix it.
Transmute it.
Bit by bit.
Until it's,
Nothing, but...
a golden
Nugget.

And I'll carry
It with pride.
Til the day
I fucking
Die!

Cause my freedom,
Didn't come free...
But neither does
My Wisdom.
And that shit's,
Fucking,
Priceless, to me.

Alchemy

There's nothing wrong with me.
There's nothing wrong with you.
Just pain, and fear, and some sorrow too.

Breath in,
Breath out.
Let. It. Go.

Alchemize that shit,
Turn it gold.
Revenge?... uh-uh.
Best served cold.

Get paid
for what they
put you through.

Let's face it,
I deserve it
& so do you.

Swinging to Steady

I can't love you
exactly as you are—
from afar?

Hunny,
you're neglecting to see
the duality.

You "agree to disagree" …

Is it because I'm right,
and that's the fallacy?
Or is it because
you don't actually understand
what I mean?

Do you like it
when I bend myself
into incomprehensible positions,
like a pretzel?

Damn,
I know I'm flexible—
but this shit
is fucking uncomfortable.

"Stop being a doormat,
and grow a backbone."
So I did.
Now, I'm "too rigid."
I need to be more loose.

And apparently,
my boundaries are always
"Lose-lose."
What the hell do I do?

I'm navigating uncharted waters
in the dark unknown,
living a life that feels
foreign at best.

Between the life I left
and the life waiting
at the end of this quest
is nothing short
of civil unrest.

Things may seem
Unsteady,
But I'm ready

Patiently waiting,
And trying my best-
Erratic pendulum,
Swinging
please find your middle
and come to rest.

Toxic Loyalty

Loyalty

Noun

A faithfulness
Unwavering in the face
Of temptation—
To renounce, desert,
Or betray.

At least, that's what
Merriam and Webster say.

This definition
Stops me in my tracks,
Forcing me to
Look back.

Cue the unraveling
Of everything I thought—
And everything I was taught—
About loyalty.

As I sit
In this Panera,
Sipping my green tea,
I try to disguise
The fact

That I just realized
All the lies
I was force-fed—

Instance after instance
Popping into my head.

No wonder my life
Has been steeped
In so much dread.

A lifelong dedication
To self-sacrifice
And self-betrayal.

Did I serve you well?
Did you appreciate
When I self-deprecate?

When I took your bait,
Which you switched
Without a hitch—

So smoothly,
So effortlessly.
You're so good at it.

No, really,
It's almost like
It comes naturally.

Toxicity,
Masked
And labeled
As loyalty.

A free hall pass,
A secret way
To betray—
And get away,
Without paying
For the twisted
Games you play.

To make me adhere
To the paradoxical
Rules you lay.

Excuse me,
I've got something to say.
I've got some
Boundaries to lay.

No longer will I
Self-betray
Or play
Your toxic games,

Just to take the blame—
To feel like
I'm going insane

For simply being me,
Living life
My own way.

Tangled Red Threads

Tangled red threads
Of old generational webs
You weave around me,
In complicated, deep-seeded patterns
You refuse to see,
Let alone believe.

Squeezing tight,
Shallowing my breath—
Slowly suffocating

Defensively,
"it's for your own good,
And protection.
You don't get it,
You won't get it,
You're not listening
You don't understand"

Fawning,
I'm trying to understand
I want understand
Help me understand

Crickets.
Here, in the silence—
It hits. Bam.

I'm Not committed to
misunderstanding you.
You're committed to
being misunderstood.

While you lay dormant.
I move in silence,
Slinking out between
The tangled red threads,
Leaving you and it be,
Behind me.

Unsure why leaving you
Hurts the way it does,
Until I look back—

I got out, I'm free.
But you're too wrapped up
In places you don't even want to be,
Too loyal to toxicity
To be free.
So you refuse to leave
And choose them over me,
Blaming me,
To cope,
for what you perceive.

So yeah, I do get it.
Can't you see?
I've too had cope with
The tangled web
Of red threads
that is CPTSD.

Bound Apart

Bound by pain
too great to heal.
Forced apart
By the pain we conceal

Between Sisters,
Wounds run deep
Sick, Twisted secrets
Forced to keep

No peace in heart
Neither together
Nor apart

I trigger you
You trigger me
Wounds long sewn shut
Get re-open up

This ain't opposites attract...
It's a karmic contract.

The Birth of Lack Mindset

I grew up believing,
I was unworthy and undeserving.
Somehow both,
Too much and not enough.

I never fit in.
I never felt
Like I belonged.
Sorta', kinda',
Like an orphan.
With a family
And a home.

From stand-in brothers,
To stand in sisters,
And mothers,
No one quite
Filled the void.
If so,
only Temporarily.

Inadvertently,
this taught me,
Security and stability
Were a luxury.
And I lived in poverty.

A Burdened Choice

A roll filled
Out of obligation.
Led to a
Lifetime of
Repercussion.

Crown unwanted
And unnatural,
Yet adorned.
Expectation exceeded.
You outperformed.

No recognition,
Received...
Only scorn.

Resignation;
Always denied.
Roll abandonment;
the ultimate crime.

Situation;
Loose – loose.
Whatever will you do?

Whatever will you choose?
Self-preservation...
Or
Others' expectations?

A recipe for Surrogate Love

2 Shots of espresso
2 Tbsp of cocoa mix
1 Pinch of Sea salt
20 oz of milk

That's the recipe to my morning coffee.
It tastes like the love my mother
Was too burdened to give me.

From the first soul-warming sip
To the last tasty drop,
Unlike hers,
It's divine
Cold or hot.

8 of Cups

Roads paved of stone.
I walk home.
With or without hope,

That one day,
It will be gone.

And what's done,
Will be done.

I'll be free from all,
Not just some.

Wasteland

Smiling,
And satiated,
I dance amongst
The ruble and ruin
I created...

A place once familiar,
Now destitute
and Desecrated.

I Destroyed it all
In my wake.
The past,
I Forsake.

Far, far from self-deprecation.
And not for self-preservation.
But, for self-salvation.

It looks barren and worn.
But...
if you were here before,
You'd see It was battered,
And war-torn.

Sometimes, what is, Nothing anymore,
Is far better than,
What was the something before.

From badland,
To wasteland.
Tracing the outline,
of what used to be.

Remembering and
Making peace
With, what
Was no longer,
good for me.

Purgatory

On this bridge,
Stuck between 2 worlds,
I sit.

On the left,
The precipice…

A new life…

The right,
My life of old,
Pain and strife.

I know this bridge
Is only temporary…

I have to choose quickly,
And the choice is scary.

Unfamiliar Comfortability?
Or
Uncomfortable familiarity?

Deep breath.
Stand tall.
Face left…

Leave. It. All.

Seasons of Alignment

Summer heat and sunshine,
Ignites the wildfire
In this untamed Leo,
Heart of mine

Autumn leaves,
Faling from branches,
They no longer need.
Shedding this tired skin,
That no longer serves me.

Winter grows cold.
Light dulls.
Hermit mode.
Death of you.
Death of me.
Death of we.
In Hibernation,
Amongst barren trees.

Spring,
The rebirth
Of mother earth.
From my cocoon,
I emerge.
Wings unfurl,
Back to reign.
Breath, Smile
For the cycle,
Has begun again.

Deep Clean

Have you ever wanted to
peel off your suit of skin?
Untie every knot
in your muscles,
Deep within?

Drain out the poison
that seeped in
staining everything
a grotesque green
Down to the bone
in which it steeped in?

Go through,
The deepest parts of you
With a fine-tooth comb,
Plucking stray hairs
of deep-rooted,
Limiting beliefs—
And let them all go.

To sew even the tiniest
of wounds shut,
Take out your
overheated brain,
Run it under ice-cold water,
Rinsing away
rumination
Till it's rendered numb.

To throw your skin suit
in the washer,
Washing away
tainted energy—
Down the drain it sinks.
Then toss it in the dryer,
Hoping, if you're lucky,
It just might shrink

It can't just be me.
If you feel the way I do,
Believe me—
You are so fucking seen.

Rat Race

Water splashing.
Cold as frost
Against,
My hot face.
From
Rushing,
In such fast pace.

Waiting
On the sun,
For summers
Heat.
Burn my cheeks,
Hot
As mace.

Isn't this always the case?
Rushing for what?
Just to win the next rat race?
What's the hurry?

To die?

What. A. life.

Sit still.
Soak it in.
One day,
It'll still end.

But we don't got to rush.
Think of what you'll miss,
If you keep living
Life like this.

You'll miss everything possible,
If you rush to the finish line,
As soon as humanly possible.

I get it we're programmed,
To win.
To be the best.
To be #1.
To be a champion.
But death isn't the race,
You wanna win first place.

It's not about being fast,
Make Evey day count.
Even if that means,
coming in last.

Bittersweet Goodbye

Being burned
By becoming what
We were running from:

My mother,
Your father—
Pain chased.

Your drug of choice:
Anything opiate-based.
Mine:
Anything pain-laced.

In that rocky bottom,
We didn't want to be,
Can never be forgotten.

Awfully scary,
In the dark unknown,
I'm glad we were lucky
And didn't have to face it alone.

Somehow,
We made the best of it
And even had a little fun.

Genuine smiles,
Even though
We were numb.

Sharing words of wisdom,
In lessons hard learned.

Seeing the light
In each other—
A beacon of hope
For which we yearned.

One step at a time,
Ruminating in our minds,
Until,
Finally,
Our own pace we'd find.

Day by day,
The darkness waned,
Taking with it
Our then-codependent
Friendship,
now strained.

Given the chance,
I wouldn't change
A single thing.

I miss you
Every day—
Since you've moved away.

I know
I wouldn't have
Made it through
Without you.

So, I'm okay
That it happened
This way.

I hope you're still
Clean,
Well,
Safe,
And okay.

I'll choose to
Remember you
This way.

Forever grateful
For the friendship
That kept us alive
In our darkest of days.

Odessey Bound

With a heavy heart,
Ways must be part.

Baggage from the past.
A cumbersome
burdensome sack.
Slung forever over shoulder,
Leaving it's carrier broken hearted
With an aching back.

Deflected upon
For far too long.
Left to fester and mold,
Now long past Fatal to hold.
The how, was lost in oblivion,
to let go.

Petulance runs dry,
Gives way to time
And an eased mind.
Occupied with the wisdom
Of The great Divine.

Ropes unraveled,
To I No longer bound.
Shedded Tattered sack
Lies discarded upon the
Ground.

Resentment in heart,
No longer to be found.
Love and forgiveness,
Abundant by the pound.

An Odyssey abound,
On exploration for
The remnants of me
yet to be found.

Put to rest,
Misplaced Conceptions
Of heads in clouds,
For I possess
Deeply rooted feet
upon the ground.

Once fully
solidified In self,
Like the earth
In relation to the sun,
I'll be back around.

Hope

Hope,
one of the most
important things in my life.

It's been my guide.
A source of light.
I cannot lie,
Without it,
 I would've died.

It's gotten me through
My worst of times yet.
Only gratitude,
Can settle the debt.

For hope knows no bounds,
Wherever you are,
It can always be found.

Grief

It can happen all at once,
In an instant,
If you're lucky.

But most of the time,
It happens bit by bit.
Over a thousand different times,
Over a thousand different days,
In a thousand different ways.

No matter if it's
Friend turned foe,
Or if it was or wasn't
Their time to go.

No matter the way,
Nothing makes it hurt less.
Quick rip band aid
Or savoring the pain,
It's all distress.

You can go with the flow,
When it comes and it goes,
Or you can wallow.
Either way,
Still leaves you feeling
Quite hallow.

No way is wrong,
But no way feels quite right.
You feel weak,
Wondering how to
Keep on keeping on.
And everyone
Just tells you to stay strong.

An isolating
Universal experience.
Pre-recorded phrases
Falling on deaf ears,
Seemingly incoherent.

Navigating this dark map,
Paths winding
and mysterious.

Searching for the way out,
Til your exhausted
And delirious.

Days blur together
Til they just become
Light and dark.
Your stuck
But still,
time carries on

Pain courses
Through your veins,
Patiently waiting
Till it's done.

Knowing what's intertwined.
And that you can't
Truly appreciate love,
Without the other one.

Gold Rush

I collect memories.
In the way, miners collect gold.

Carefully sifting and straining,
Sure to get, every. Last. Speck.

Good or bad,
It don't really matter.

Capturing, observing,
Inspecting, restoring,
Polishing, & hoarding

Gold or pyrite,
It don't really matter.

To stubborn to let any of em' go
Forever in my heart to hold,
Worth their weight in gold.

Release

Sensory Deprived
Alone in my room,
Snuggled comfy
In my blanket cocoon.

Breathing steady,
Feeling the rise and fall,
With eyes closed—

Until what my body
Keeps hidden
Shows.

Wave after wave,
Allowing its flow,

Bubbling to the surface—
The lump in my throat
Grows.

Icy and hot, evaporating
Off my back
As it goes.

Layer by layer,
My body's score
Is getting low,

As I release
The pain and tension
From my trauma and woes.

Staying grounded and strong,
Reaping what I did not sow.

This is how I heal.
This is how I grow.
And I do it all on my own.

Radiate

Radiate love.
Radiate positivity.
Radiate light.
Radiate you.

It will radiate back,
times 2.

Confetti Soul

Just as confetti
Scatters and blows,
So do pieces of our soul.

We leave them
Here and there
Wherever, we may go.

We leave them
In hugs,
And handshakes,
And in kind words, too.

In kisses,
And wishes,
And I love you's.

We leave them in
Shops,
And on trains,
And planes.

In cars,
And parks,
And yes…
Even bars.

But mostly,
We leave them in
The hearts and souls
Of others,
Near and far.

Lady willow

Like grandmother willow tree,
A wise woman too,
lives in me.

Speaking in
Riddles & rhymes,
That I have to decipher,
most of the time.

Sometimes stern,
But always kind.

Keeping me going
On this path of mine.
Reminding me of my light:
"Never dim, dear.
 Always shine"

A Wounded Healer's Destiny

A yearning,
for understanding.

Feelings felt
Thousands of feet deep,
The epitome of
Empathy.

Hands warm,
And healing,
On the burdened backs
Of the grieving.

It's a gift,
A curse,
A lesson,
And truly, a
Profound Blessing.

A Sense of Completion

In a weird way
I'm thankful.

Not for the pain,
But the lessons
Learned,

And the strength,
Resiliency, and wisdom
Gained.

The golden gifts, I'm left with

The ability ...
To See the beauty
In the everyday,
No matter what,
May come my way.

To allow emotion
To ebb and flow,
Without drowning
In the wave.

To choose myself,
Without guilt and shame.

To love myself,
Without feeling
Conceded or vain.

To take up space,
Without thinking
I'm in the way.

To set boundaries
And protect my peace,
Without the need
To people-please.

To attach and detach securely,
Without falling into
co-dependency.

To allow my light to shine,
Without the need to dim Or hide.

To accept praise and help,
Without feeling undeserving
Or unworthy.

To trust myself wholeheartedly,
Without ruminating indecisively.

To use the gift of discernment properly,
Without chasing butterflies
Or familiarity.

To succeed and persevere,
Without fear of failure
Or self-sabotaging.

To Manifest and listen
to my intuition faithfully,
Without lack mindset blocking me.

To use my voice,
Without compliancy
To forced silency.

To be free to be me,
Authentically
And unapologetically.

To create my own life
And handcraft.
It beautifully.

Dear,
Anyone offended

You are deserving
and worthy
Of healing
And being heard too.
No one.
No thing.
Is stopping you.

If the shoe doesn't fit,
Don't force it.
And if it does...
Well, if you're not changing it
Then you're choosing it.

So choose wisely,
And change often.

Epilogue

I don't hold anything against my family. Everything that happened has been long forgiven. It was unfathomably hard for everyone involved, not just me. Each one of us fought like hell to survive and we all got out. For that, I'm incredibly proud of us.

Our family has lasting impacts of the past. I mean... How can we not?
We aren't perfect and we never will be and that's ok. However, without a doubt, I can say that whether things are good or not we love each other immensely in our own way and we always will.

As far as my abuser, in the past I've tried to forgive her because I thought I had to, to be "fully healed". I don't know if I can say that I've forgiven her and I can't say for sure if I ever will. Some things are unforgivable and that's ok. It doesn't define my "healed-ness".

I have let it all go, though. I can acknowledge that hurt people hurt people and no well person would do that to someone. I can assume those things probably happened to her as well. I have an understanding of that but at the end of the day the understanding doesn't change much for me and it doesn't excuse what happened. I can say that I no longer harbor hate. I'm in a place of ambivalence and I'm quite content here.

I once told my therapist, after sharing some parts of this, that the day I ever gain the courage to release this, That's the day I know I'm healed "enough". That day is here and I feel that sentiment so deeply. I'm proud of myself for doing all the soul-ripping, heart-wrenching, hard work it took me to get here to the place I am now. It was the hardest thing I've ever done. I'm so glad I didn't give up. There were so many times I wanted to. There were moments that felt impossible to make it through let alone come out the other side of.

My journey has led me to my long-suppressed self. I may have lost people, places, and things along the way but I've found so much more. I've found happiness and peace, my voice, and... me. I will forever continue to walk on the path of self-growth. I'm committed to being the best me I can be. For now, I'm celebrating the me I am now and how far I've come.

www.ingramcontent.com/pod-product-compliance
Lightning Source LLC
LaVergne TN
LVHW010553070526
838199LV00063BA/4961